DEVOTIONS
FOR
CONFIDENCE
&INTEGRITY

HEBREWS & 1 JOHN

DEVOTIONS
FOR
CONFIDENCE
&INTEGRITY

HEBREWS & 1 JOHN

Warren W. Wiersbe

HONOR HB BOOKS

Inspiration and Motivation for the Seasons of Life

COOK COMMUNICATIONS MINISTRIES
Colorado Springs, Colorado • Paris, Ontario
KINGSWAY COMMUNICATIONS LTD
Eastbourne, England

Honor Books® is an imprint of
Cook Communications Ministries, Colorado Springs, CO 80918
Cook Communications, Paris, Ontario
Kingsway Communications, Eastbourne, England

DEVOTIONS FOR CONFIDENCE AND INTEGRITY
© 2006 by Warren W. Wiersbe

Cover Design: Jackson Design CO, LLC/Greg Jackson

First Printing, 2006
Printed in the United States of America

1 2 3 4 5 6 7 8 9 10 Printing/Year 10 09 08 07 06

Unless otherwise noted, Scripture quotations are taken from the HOLY BIBLE, NEW INTERNATIONAL VERSION®. Copyright © 1973, 1978, 1984 by International Bible Society. Used by permission of Zondervan. All rights reserved. Scripture quotations marked (KJV) are taken from the King James Version of the Bible. (Public Domain.) Italics in Scripture have been added by the author for emphasis.

This book was originally published as two paperback editions in 1994 and 1995, compiled by Stan Campbell. Each devotional reading is adapted from Warren Wiersbe's "Be" series.

Library of Congress Cataloging-in-Publication Data

Wiersbe, Warren W.
  Devotions for confidence and integrity : Hebrews and 1 John / Warren Wiersbe.
      p. cm. -- (60 days in the Word)
  Includes bibliographical references and index.
  ISBN 1-56292-703-5 (alk. paper)
  1. Bible. N.T. Hebrews--Meditations. 2. Confidence--Religious aspects--Christianity--Meditations. 3. Bible. N.T. Epistle of John, 1st--Meditations. 4. Integrity--Religious aspects--Christianity--Meditations. I. Title.

BS2775.54.W54 2006
242'.2--dc22
                                                          2005026495

Confidence

Thirty Daily Readings from the Book of Hebrews

Have you noticed how often the words "confident" and "confidence" show up in contemporary advertising?

Automobile manufacturers tell us we can drive their products with confidence because the designers have built into the vehicles the latest safety features. (Wouldn't it be nice to have safety features in our daily lives?)

Pharmaceutical firms announce that we can use their latest cold medications with confidence because they will take away the cold symptoms but won't make us drowsy. (They can't cure the cold, but that's another story.)

Publishers assure us we can read their newspapers and magazines with confidence because they print only the truth—the facts—and nobody has ever caught them in a lie.

Confidence is a matter of trust. In fact, that's what the word means: "to trust." Everybody lives by faith in something, *and our faith is only as good as the person or the thing we are trusting*. Do you have confidence in the object of your faith?

The epistle to the Hebrews is about faith in Jesus Christ, the Son of God. It is one of three books in the New Testament written to explain one Old Testament verse of Scripture: "The righteous will live by his faith" (Hab. 2:4). The epistle to the Romans explains who "the righteous" are; the epistle to the Galatians describes how they "live"; and the epistle to the Hebrews tells us what it means to live "by faith."

When we learn to live "by faith," we have confidence and are not blown over by every wind that comes along (Eph. 4:14). All Christians know what Jesus Christ did on earth, but the epistle to the Hebrews tells us what Jesus Christ is doing for His people *right now in heaven*.

What a difference it makes when we trust Him for *everything* and have confidence in His promises and His power.

The epistle to the Hebrews relates how God takes ordinary people and helps them face tremendous challenges and do incredible things because *they have confidence in Him.* Once you understand what Jesus Christ is doing for you in heaven today, your own confidence will grow, your life will be transformed, and you will know the joy and excitement of living by faith.

Day 1

Hear and Now

❦

Read Hebrews 1

In the past God spoke to our forefathers through the prophets at many times and in various ways, but in these last days he has spoken to us by his Son.
HEBREWS 1:1–2

A man from Leeds, England, visited his doctor to have his hearing checked. The doctor removed the man's hearing aid, and the patient's hearing immediately improved! He had been wearing the device *in the wrong ear* for more than twenty years!

I once asked a pastor friend, "Do you have a deaf ministry in your church?" He replied, "There are times when I think the whole church needs a deaf ministry—they just don't seem to hear me."

There is a difference between merely *listening* and truly *hearing*. Jesus often cried, "He who has ears to hear, let him hear!" This statement suggests that it takes more than physical ears to hear the voice of God. It also requires a receptive heart.

Many people have avoided the epistle to the Hebrews and, consequently, have robbed themselves of practical spiritual help. Some have avoided this book because they are "afraid of it." The "warnings" in Hebrews have made them uneasy. Others have avoided this book because they think it is "too difficult" for the average Bible student. To be sure, there are some profound truths in Hebrews, and no preacher or teacher would dare to claim to know them all! But the general message of the book is clear, and there is no reason why you and I should not understand and profit from it.

❧

Applying God's Truth:

1. When you go to church, what percent of the time would you say you are truly *hearing* as opposed to *merely* listening?

2. How can you hear more clearly, given that God "has spoken to us by his Son"?

3. What do you hope to accomplish through your readings from the book of Hebrews?

Day 2

A Downward Cycle

Read Hebrews 2:1

We must pay more careful attention, therefore, to what we have heard, so that we do not drift away.

HEBREWS 2:1

If we do not listen to God's Word and really *hear* it, we will start to *drift*. Neglect always leads to drifting, in things material and physical as well as spiritual. As we drift from the Word, we start to *doubt* the Word because *faith* comes by hearing the Word of God (Rom. 10:17 KJV). We start to get hard hearts, and this leads to spiritual sluggishness, which produces *dullness* toward the Word. We become "dull of hearing" (Matt. 13:15 KJV)—lazy listeners! This leads to a *despiteful* attitude toward the Word to the extent that we willfully *disobey* God, and this gradually develops into a *defiant* attitude—we almost "dare" God to do anything!

Now what does God do while this spiritual regression is going on? He keeps speaking to us, encouraging us to get back to the Word. If we fail to listen and obey, then He begins to chasten us. This chastening process is the theme of Hebrews 12, the climactic chapter in the epistle. "The Lord will judge *his people*" (Heb. 10:30). God does not allow His children to become "spoiled brats" by permitting them willfully to defy His Word. He always chastens in love (Rev. 3:19 KJV).

❧

Applying God's Truth:

1. Can you recall a time when you were caught in the drifting-doubting-dullness-despising-disobeying-defying cycle? What was the lowest level you reached? How did you break out of the downward spiral?

2. How can you keep from beginning to drift in the first place?

3. Have you ever experienced God's loving chastening? In what ways?

Day 3

Streams of Mercy

❧

Read Hebrews 2:2–3

> *For if the message spoken by angels was binding ...*
> *how shall we escape if we ignore such a great salvation?*
> HEBREWS 2:2–3

The next time you sing "Come, Thou Fount of Every Blessing," recall that the composer, Robert Robinson, was converted under the mighty preaching of George Whitefield, but that later he drifted from the Lord. He had been greatly used as a pastor, but neglect of spiritual things led him astray. In an attempt to find peace he began to travel. During one of his journeys, he met a young woman who was evidently very spiritually minded.

"What do you think of this hymn I have been reading?" she asked Robinson, handing him the book. *It was his own hymn!* He tried to avoid her question but it was hopeless, for the Lord was speaking to him. Finally, he broke down and confessed who he was and how he had been living away from the Lord.

"But these 'streams of mercy' are still flowing," the woman assured him; and through her encouragement Robinson was restored to fellowship with the Lord.

It is easy to drift with the current, but it is difficult to return against the stream. Our salvation is a "great salvation," purchased at a great price. It brings with it great promises and blessings, and it leads to a great inheritance in glory. How can we neglect it?

❀

Applying God's Truth:

1. In what ways are God's "streams of mercy" flowing through your life?

2. When was a recent time you experienced great difficulty "going against the current" in order to follow God when no one else seemed to want to do so?

3. In what way is yours a "great salvation"?

Day 4

Sins of the Saints

꧁꧂

Read Hebrews 2:3–9

This salvation, which was first announced by the Lord,
was confirmed to us by those who heard him.
HEBREWS 2:3

We have the idea that believers today "under grace" can escape the chastening hand of God that was so evident "under law." But "unto whomsoever much is given, of him shall be much required" (Luke 12:48 KJV). Not only have we received the Word from the Son of God, but that Word has been confirmed by "signs, wonders and various miracles, and gifts of the Holy Spirit distributed according to his will" (Heb. 2:4). The phrase "signs and wonders" is found eleven times in the New Testament. Here it refers to the miracles that witnessed to the Word and gave confirmation that it was true. These miracles were performed by the apostles. Today we have the completed Word of God, so there is no need for these apostolic miracles. God now bears witness through His Spirit using the Word. The Spirit also gives spiritual gifts to God's people so that they may minister in the church (1 Cor. 12:1–11).

I have often told the story about the pastor who preached a series of sermons on "the sins of the saints." He was severely reprimanded by one of the members of the church. "After all," said the member, "sin in the lives of Christians is different from sin in the lives of other people."

"Yes," replied the pastor, "it's *worse!*"

⚜

Applying God's Truth:

1. If a stranger were to ask you today, "Why do you believe in God?" what reasons would you give?

2. What are some of the gifts of the Holy Spirit that you feel have been "distributed" to you? Be specific.

3. Do you agree that sin in the lives of Christians is worse than sin in the lives of other people? Why?

Day 5

Mercy and Faithfulness

❧

Read Hebrews 2:10–18

*For this reason [Jesus] had to be made like his brothers in every way,
in order that he might become a merciful and faithful high priest in service to
God, and that he might make atonement for the sins of the people.*

HEBREWS 2:17

If you want an example of a man who was *not* a merciful and faithful high priest, then read the biblical account of Eli (1 Sam. 2:27–36). Here was a high priest who did not even lead his own sons into a faithful walk with God. Eli even accused brokenhearted Hannah of being drunk (1:9–18)!

Jesus Christ is both merciful and faithful; He is merciful toward people and faithful toward God. He can never fail in His priestly ministries. He made the necessary sacrifice for our sins so that we might be reconciled to God. He did not need to make a sacrifice for Himself because He is sinless.

But what happens when we who have been saved are tempted to sin? He stands ready to help us! He was tempted when He was on earth, but no temptation ever conquered Him (Heb. 4:14–15). Because He has defeated every enemy, He is able to give us the grace we need to overcome temptation (v. 16). The word translated "succour" in the King James Version (or "help" in the New International Version) in Hebrews 2:18 literally means "to run to the cry of a child." It means "to bring help when it is needed." Angels are able to serve us (1:14), but they are not able to "succour" us in our times of temptation. Only Jesus Christ can do that, and He can do it because He became a man and suffered and died for us.

❧

Applying God's Truth:

1. What are some specific ways that Jesus has been merciful to you lately? In so doing, how has He been faithful toward God?

2. List all the temptations you have faced during the past week.

3. For each of the temptations you listed, how would you like Jesus to help you stand firmly against it?

Day 6

Two Good Examples

Read Hebrews 3:1–11

> *Fix your thoughts on Jesus, the apostle and high priest*
> *whom we confess. He was faithful to the one who appointed him,*
> *just as Moses was faithful in all God's house.*
>
> HEBREWS 3:1–2

Jesus Christ is not only the Apostle; He is also the High Priest. Moses was a prophet who on occasion served as a high priest. That title belonged to his brother Aaron. In fact, Jesus Christ has the title "great high priest" (4:14).

As the Apostle, Jesus Christ represented God to people, and as the High Priest, He now represents people to God in heaven. Moses, of course, fulfilled similar ministries; for he taught Israel God's truth, and he prayed for Israel when he met God on the mount (Ex. 32:30–32). Moses was primarily the prophet of the law, while Jesus Christ is the messenger of God's grace (John 1:17). Moses helped prepare the way for the coming of the Savior to earth.

However, the writer of Hebrews notes that Moses and Jesus Christ were both faithful in the work God gave them to do. Moses was not sinless, as was Jesus Christ, but he was faithful and obeyed God's will (Num. 12:7). This would be an encouragement to those first-century Jewish believers to remain faithful to Christ, even in the midst of the tough trials they were experiencing. Instead of going back to Moses, they should *imitate* Moses and be faithful in their calling.

❧

Applying God's Truth:

1. How does Jesus serve as an apostle ("one sent with a commission")? How does He serve as your *High Priest?*

2. How might your spiritual life improve if you were to imitate the faithfulness of Moses? How might you better imitate Christ?

3. Specifically, what are some things you can do to "fix your thoughts on Jesus"?

Day 7

Heart Problems

✦

Read Hebrews 3:12–19

> *See to it, brothers, that none of you has a sinful, unbelieving*
> *heart that turns away from the living God. But encourage one another daily*
> *... so that none of you may be hardened by sin's deceitfulness.*
> HEBREWS 3:12–13

The heart of every problem is a problem in the heart. The people of Israel (except Moses, Joshua, and Caleb) erred in their hearts, which means that their hearts wandered from God and His Word. They also had evil hearts of unbelief; they did not believe that God would give them victory in Canaan. They had seen God perform great signs in Egypt, yet they doubted He was adequate for the challenge of Canaan (vv. 7–11, 16–19).

When a person has an *erring* heart and a *disbelieving* heart, the result will also be a *hard* heart. This is a heart that is insensitive to the Word and work of God. So hard was the heart of Israel that the people even wanted to return to Egypt (Num. 14:1–4)! Imagine wanting to exchange their freedom under God for slavery in Egypt! Of course, all this history spoke to the hearts of the readers of this letter, because they were in danger of "going back" themselves.

Believers who doubt God's Word and rebel against Him do not miss heaven, but they do miss out on the blessing of their inheritance today, and they must suffer the chastening of God.

⚜

Applying God's Truth:

1. When was the last time your heart was "hardened by sin's deceitfulness"?

2. What are some blessings we stand to lose if we don't deal with hard-heartedness?

3. We are commanded to "encourage one another daily." How do you think this helps prevent forming a "hard heart" toward God? Whom have you encouraged today?

Day 8

A Lesson in Geography

❦

Read Hebrews 4

> *Since the promise of entering [God's] rest still stands, let us be careful*
> *that none of you be found to have fallen short of it.*
> HEBREWS 4:1

We must understand that there are spiritual lessons in the geography of Israel's experiences. The nation's bondage in Egypt is an illustration of sinners' bondage in this world. Much as Israel was delivered from Egypt by the blood of lambs and the power of God, so sinners who believe on Christ are delivered from the bondage of sin.

It was not God's will that Israel remain either in Egypt or in the wilderness. His desire was that the people enter their glorious inheritance in the land of Canaan. But when the Israelites got to the border of their inheritance, they delayed because they doubted the promise of God (Num. 13—14). "We are not able," wept the ten spies and the people (13:31–33; 14:1–4). "We are able with God's help!" said Moses, Joshua, and Caleb (13:30; 14:5–9). Because the people went backward in unbelief instead of forward by faith, they missed their inheritance and died in the wilderness.

What does Canaan represent to us as Christians today? It represents our spiritual inheritance in Christ. Israel had to cross the Jordan River by faith (a picture of believers as they die to self and the world). They had to step out by faith (Josh. 1:3) and claim the land for themselves, just as believers today must do.

❦

Applying God's Truth:

1. Do you feel that you are "in bondage" in any way? How might faith help you experience real freedom?

2. Do you ever want, even briefly, to return to the lifestyle you had before becoming a Christian? If so, why? How do you deal with such feelings?

3. What do you think it means to enter God's rest?

Day 9

The Right to Serve

❧

Read Hebrews 5:1–6

Every high priest is selected from among men and is appointed to represent
them in matters related to God, to offer gifts and sacrifices for sins....
No one takes this honor upon himself; he must be called by God.

HEBREWS 5:1, 4

When I became pastor of the Calvary Baptist Church in
Covington, Kentucky, it was necessary for me to go to the city
hall and be bonded. Otherwise, I would not have the authority to perform marriages. I had to show my ordination certificate and prove that
I was indeed ministering at the church.

One day I received a frantic phone call from one of our members.
Some Christian friends were being married the next day by a relative
from Michigan, and they discovered that he was not authorized to
perform the ceremony! Could I help them? The visiting pastor could
read the ceremony as well as I could, and he knew the couple better
than I did; but he lacked the authority to minister.

No man could appoint himself as a priest, let alone *high* priest.
The very existence of a priesthood and a system of sacrifices gave
evidence that people were estranged from God. It was an act of
grace on God's part that He instituted the whole Levitical system.
Today, that system is fulfilled in the ministry of Jesus Christ. He is
both the Sacrifice and the High Priest who ministers to God's
people on the basis of His once-for-all offering on the cross.

⚜

Applying God's Truth:

1. How was Jesus given "authority to minister" in His role as High Priest?

2. What requests do you need to make of Jesus today specifically in regard to His High Priestly duties?

3. What makes Jesus the ideal High Priest to represent us before God?

Day 10

Superior Sympathy

❧

Read Hebrews 5:7–8

During the days of Jesus' life on earth, he offered up prayers and petitions with loud cries and tears to the one who could save him from death, and he was heard because of his reverent submission. Although he was a son, he learned obedience from what he suffered.

HEBREWS 5:7–8

E very Old Testament high priest had to minister to people who were "ignorant and … going astray" (v. 2). God made no provision but judgment for the high-handed sins of rebellion. But He did make provision when people sinned through ignorance or weakness. An Old Testament priest could identify with the sinners since he himself was a sinner. In fact, on the Day of Atonement, the high priest had to offer a sacrifice for himself before he could offer one for the nation (Lev. 16; Heb. 9:7)!

We would think that one sinner would have compassion for another sinner, but this is not always the case. Sin makes people selfish. Sin can blind us to the hurts of others. Sin can harden our hearts and make us judgmental instead of sympathetic. Remember how heartbroken Hannah, who was praying for a son, was accused by High Priest Eli of being drunk (1 Sam. 1:9–18)? And when King David was confronted with a story of a rich man's sin, he had no sympathy for him, even though David himself was a worse sinner (2 Sam. 12).

No, it is the spiritually minded person with a clean heart who sympathizes with sinners and seeks to help them. Because we are so sinful, we have a hard time helping other sinners; but because Jesus is perfect, He is able to meet our needs after we sin (Heb. 4:15–16).

Applying God's Truth:

1. On a scale of 1 (least) to 10 (most), what would you say is your average level of compassion shown toward the sinful people with whom you come into contact?

2. What can you learn from Jesus' example of "reverent submission"? Be specific.

3. Is your status as "child of God" something you have begun to take for granted or, like Jesus, do you strive to continue to learn obedience from your sufferings?

Day 11

No Reputation

Read Hebrews 5:9–10

> *Once made perfect, [Jesus] became the source of*
> *eternal salvation for all who obey him.*
>
> HEBREWS 5:9

No matter what trials we meet, Jesus Christ is able to understand our needs and help us. We need never doubt His ability to sympathize and strengthen. It is also worth noting that sometimes God puts *us* through difficulties so that we might better understand the needs of others and become able to encourage them.

When Charles Haddon Spurgeon was a young preacher in London, his successful ministry aroused the envy of some of the clergy, and they attacked him with various kinds of slander and gossip. His sermons were called "trashy," and he was called "an actor" and "a pulpit buffoon." Even after his ministry was established, Spurgeon was lied about in the press (including the *religious* press), and this was bound to discourage him.

After one particularly scurrilous report in the press, Spurgeon fell before the Lord and prayed, "O Lord Jesus, Thou didst make Thyself of no reputation for me. I willingly lay my reputation down for Thy sake." From that time on, Spurgeon had peace in his heart. He knew that his Great High Priest understood his need and would give him the grace he needed for each hour.

‹❈›

Applying God's Truth:

1. What trials are you facing today in which Jesus is the only person who can help you?

2. Have you ever been so devoted to Jesus (and your own spiritual growth) that your reputation or motives were called into question by others? If so, how did you respond?

3. Try to recall a difficulty you once faced, after which you were able to minister effectively to someone else facing the same or a similar problem. How did you feel to be able to help someone based on your previous personal experience?

Day 12

Spiritual Senses

❧

Read Hebrews 5:11–14

> *Anyone who lives on milk, being still an infant, is not acquainted with the teaching about righteousness. But solid food is for the mature.*
> HEBREWS 5:13–14

Just as our physical bodies have senses, without which we could not function, so our inner "spiritual man" has "spiritual senses." As we feed on the Word of God, and apply it in daily life, our inner "spiritual senses" get their exercise and become strong and keen. Paul called this process training ourselves to be godly (1 Tim. 4:7–8).

The ability to discern good and evil is a vital part of Christian maturity. The nation of Israel in Moses' day lacked this discernment and failed to claim its promised inheritance. The readers of this letter were in danger of making the same mistake. It is impossible to stand still in the Christian life: Either we go forward and claim God's blessing, or we go backward and wander about aimlessly.

I once heard a preacher say, "Most Christians are 'betweeners.'"

"What do you mean by that?" I asked.

"They are between Egypt and Canaan—out of the place of danger, but not yet into the place of rest and rich inheritance," he replied. "They are between Good Friday and Easter Sunday—saved by the blood, but not yet enjoying newness of resurrection life."

Are *you* a "betweener"?

Applying God's Truth:

1. At what level of spiritual understanding would you say you are: (a) milk/liquid diet, (b) baby food, (c) junk food, (d) soft foods, or (e) steak and potatoes? Explain.

2. On a scale where 1 is "Egypt" and 10 is "Canaan," where would you place your spiritual progress? Are you moving forward at this point in your spiritual journey?

3. What are some ways you train yourself to distinguish between good and evil?

Day 13

Drop Anchor

Read Hebrews 6

> *We have this hope as an anchor for the soul, firm and secure.*
> *It enters the inner sanctuary behind the curtain, where Jesus,*
> *who went before us, has entered on our behalf.*

HEBREWS 6:19–20

Our hope in Christ is like an anchor for the soul. The anchor was a popular symbol in the early church. At least sixty-six pictures of anchors have been found in the catacombs. The Greek Stoic philosopher Epictetus wrote: "One must not tie a ship to a single anchor, nor life to a single hope." Christians have but one anchor—Jesus Christ our hope (Col. 1:5; 1 Tim. 1:1; Heb. 6:19).

However, this spiritual anchor is different from material anchors on ships. For one thing, we are anchored *upward*—to heaven—not downward. We are anchored, not to stand still, but *to move ahead!* Our anchor is "firm"—it cannot break—and "secure"—it cannot slip. No earthly anchor can give that kind of security!

The writer then clinches the argument: This Savior is our "forerunner." The Old Testament high priest was not a forerunner because nobody could follow him into the Holy of Holies. But Jesus Christ has gone ahead to heaven so that one day we may follow!

Applying God's Truth:

1. In what ways would you say Jesus is your "anchor"?

2. What are some areas of your life that aren't anchored as securely as you wish they were?

3. What are some ways that being anchored to Jesus has helped you *move ahead?*

Day 14

What's in a Name?

❧

Read Hebrews 7:1–2

Melchizedek was king of Salem and priest of God Most High.... First, his name means "king of righteousness"; then also, "king of Salem" means "king of peace."
HEBREWS 7:1–2

In the Bible, names and their meanings are often important. We name our children today without much consideration for what their names mean, but this was not the case in Bible days. Sometimes, a great spiritual crisis was the occasion for changing a person's name (Gen. 32:24–32; John 1:35–42).

The name "Melchizedek" means "king of righteousness" in the Hebrew language. The word "Salem" means "peace" (the Hebrew word *shalom*), so that Melchizedek is "king of peace" as well as "king of righteousness."

"Righteousness" and "peace" are often found together in Scripture. In Psalm 85:10, for example, we are told: "Righteousness and peace kiss each other." And God's purpose for His people is that they produce "a harvest of righteousness and peace" (Heb. 12:10–11).

True peace can be experienced only on the basis of righteousness. If we want to enjoy "peace with God," we must be "justified through faith" (Rom. 5:1). We cannot produce righteousness by keeping the Old Testament law (Gal. 2:21). It is only through the work of Jesus Christ on the cross that righteousness and peace can "kiss each other."

◦⋆⋆⋆◦

Applying God's Truth:

1. What do you think would be an appropriate "biblical" name for you (such as "king of peace" or "king of righteousness")?

2. In what ways is Jesus your King of peace?

3. In what ways is Jesus your King of righteousness?

Day 15

Without Genealogy

Read Hebrews 7:3–28

Without father or mother, without genealogy, without beginning of days or end of life, like the Son of God [Melchizedek] remains a priest forever.

HEBREWS 7:3

Melchizedek was a man, so he had to have had a mother and a father. But there is no *record* of his genealogy (descent) in the Old Testament; this is significant because most great persons in the Old Testament have their ancestry identified. It was especially important that the priests be able to prove their ancestry. Here the writer of Hebrews uses an argument from silence, but it is a valid one.

Melchizedek was not an angel or some superhuman creature, nor was he an Old Testament appearance of Jesus Christ. He was a real man, a real king, and a real priest in a real city. But as far as the record is concerned, he was not born, nor did he die. In this way, he is a picture of the Lord Jesus Christ, the eternal Son of God. Though Jesus Christ did die, Calvary was not the end; for He arose from the dead and today he lives in "the power of an indestructible life" (v. 16). Since there is no account of Melchizedek's death, as far as the record is concerned, it seems that Melchizedek is still serving as a priest and king. This is another way in which he is like the eternal Son of God.

The application is clear: Neither Aaron nor any of his descendants could claim to be "without genealogy." They could not claim to have an eternal ministry. Nor could they claim to be both kings and priests, like Jesus Christ.

❧

Applying God's Truth:

1. How might your life be different if you had no knowledge of your father or mother? What things might you do differently?

2. How important is your genealogy to you? Why?

3. Why is it significant that Jesus "remains a priest forever"?

Day 16

A Seat of Honor

Read Hebrews 8:1–6

*We do have such a high priest, who sat down at the right hand
of the throne of the Majesty in heaven, and who serves in the sanctuary,
the true tabernacle set up by the Lord, not by man.*

HEBREWS 8:1–2

Today our Lord is *seated* because His work is completed. There were no chairs in the Old Testament tabernacle because the work of the priests was never finished. Each repeated sacrifice was only a reminder that none of the sacrifices ever provided a finished salvation. The blood of animals did not wash away sin or cleanse the guilty conscience; it only covered sin until that day when Jesus Christ died to take away the sin of the world (John 1:29).

Jesus Christ is not just "seated." It is *where* He is seated that adds glory to His person and His work. He is seated on the throne in heaven, at the right hand of the Father. This great truth was introduced early in this epistle (Heb. 1:3), and it will be mentioned again (10:12; 12:2). This enthronement was the fulfillment of the Father's promise to the Son, "Sit at my right hand until I make your enemies a footstool for your feet" (Ps. 110:1; Heb. 1:13). Not only did the high priest of Israel never sit down, but he never sat down on a throne. Only a priest "in the order of Melchizedek" could be enthroned, for Melchizedek was both king and priest.

❦

Applying God's Truth:

1. With all the turbulence in this world, what shows you that Jesus' work is actually completed?

2. As you think of Jesus seated in heaven, what are some assurances you feel related to the work He has finished?

3. What do you find significant about the fact that Jesus is seated on a throne?

Day 17

Short-Term Memory

❧

Read Hebrews 8:7–12

I will forgive their wickedness and will remember their sins no more.
HEBREWS 8:12

What does it mean that God remembers our sins no more? This important statement is made again in 10:17. Does it mean that our all-knowing God can actually *forget* what we have done? If God forgot anything, He would cease to be God! The phrase "remember [our] sins no more" means "hold our sins against us no more." God recalls what we have done, but He does not hold it against us (2 Cor. 5:18–19). He deals with us on the basis of grace and mercy, not law and merit. Once sin has been forgiven, it is never brought before us again. The matter is settled eternally.

As a pastor in counseling ministry, I have often heard people say, "Well, I can forgive—but I cannot forget!"

"Of course you can't forget," I usually reply. "The more you try to put this thing out of your mind, the more you will remember it. But that isn't what it means to forget." Then I go on to explain that "to forget" means "not to hold it against the person who has wronged us." We may remember what others have done, but we treat them *as though they never did it.*

How is this possible? It is possible because of the cross, for there God treated His Son *as though He had done it!* Our experience of forgiveness from God makes it possible for us to forgive others.

❧

Applying God's Truth:

1. Which of your sins stand out in your mind as those for which you are most thankful that God remembers no more?

2. Because God so readily forgives and forgets our confessed sins, how do you keep from taking His forgiveness for granted?

3. What are some recent situations in which you had the opportunity to forgive another person's offense against you, yet for some reason chose not to do so? Are you satisfied that you did the right thing, or do you need to reevaluate some of those decisions/attitudes?

Day 18

Hand in Hand

Read Hebrews 8:13

*By calling this covenant "new," he has made the first one obsolete;
and what is obsolete and aging will soon disappear.*

HEBREWS 8:13

The emphasis in the new covenant is on God's "I will." The nation of Israel at Sinai said, "Everything the LORD has said we will do" (Ex. 24:3). But they did not obey God's words. It is one thing to *say,* "We will!" and quite another to do it. But the new covenant does not depend on people's faithfulness to God but on God's faithful promise to people. The writer of Hebrews affirms God's "I will" on behalf of those who trust Jesus Christ. In fact, God's "I will" is stated three times in Hebrews 8:10 and six times in verses 8 through 12.

God led Israel out of Egypt the way a father would take his children by the hand and lead them. God gave Israel His holy law for their own good, to separate them from the other nations and to protect them from the sinful practices of the heathens around them. But the nation failed. God's responses to Israel's disobedience were to discipline them repeatedly and finally to send them into captivity.

God did not find fault with His covenant, but with His people. The problem is not with the law, but with our sinful natures, for by ourselves we cannot keep God's law. The law "made nothing perfect" (7:19) because it could not change any human heart. Only God's grace can do that.

Applying God's Truth:

1. In what ways does God lead you as a father might lead a child?

2. If God did not find fault with the "old" covenant, why did He provide a new one?

3. How do you think the old covenant "will soon disappear"?

Day 19

Internal Changes

Read Hebrews 9:1–14

> *The blood of goats and bulls ... [will] sanctify them so that they are outwardly clean. How much more, then, will the blood of Christ, who through the eternal Spirit offered himself unblemished to God, cleanse our consciences from acts that lead to death, so that we may serve the living God!*
>
> HEBREWS 9:13–14

The old covenant rituals could not change people's hearts. This is not to say that worshippers did not have a spiritual experience if their hearts trusted God, but it does mean that the emphasis was on the external ceremonial cleansing. So long as the worshippers obeyed the prescribed regulations, they were declared clean. It was "the purifying of the flesh," but not the cleansing of the conscience.

We learned from Hebrews 8 that the ministry of the new covenant is *internal*: "I will put my laws in their minds and write them on their hearts" (v. 10). This work is done by the Holy Spirit of God. But the Spirit could not dwell within us if Jesus Christ had not paid for our sins. Cleansing our consciences cannot be done by some external ceremony; it demands an internal power. Because Jesus Christ is "unblemished," He was able to offer the perfect sacrifice.

Applying God's Truth:

1. How might you have felt as an Old Testament believer, using

animal blood in your worship ceremonies? Why do you think blood was chosen as a symbol of worship?

2. How do you feel knowing that your religion still depends on blood—the blood of Jesus shed on your behalf? Do you ever have problems explaining this issue in your twenty-first-century conversations?

3. To what extent are you certain that internal changes have taken place in your life?

Day 20

Better Than Man Made

Read Hebrews 9:15–28

For Christ did not enter a man-made sanctuary that was only a copy of the true one; he entered heaven itself, now to appear for us in God's presence.
HEBREWS 9:24

New covenant Christians have *reality!* We are not depending on a high priest on earth who annually visits the Holy of Holies in a temporary sanctuary. We depend on the heavenly High Priest who has entered once and for all into the eternal sanctuary. There He represents us before God, and He *always will* (vv. 24–26).

Beware of trusting anything for your spiritual life that is "man-made." It will not last. The tabernacle was replaced by Solomon's temple, and that temple was destroyed by the Babylonians in 586 BC. When the Jews returned to their land after the Babylonian captivity, they rebuilt their temple; and King Herod, in later years, expanded and embellished it. But the Romans destroyed that temple in AD 70, and it has never been rebuilt.

Furthermore, since the genealogical records have been lost or destroyed, the Jews are not certain who can minister as priests. These things that are "man-made" are perishable, but the things not made with hands are eternal (2 Cor. 4:18).

Applying God's Truth:

1. What are some man-made items you find valuable in your worship of God?

2. We know that *what* Jesus did as our High Priest is extremely important, but what is equally important about *where* He ministers?

3. What are some unseen, eternal things you value?

Day 21

A Perfect Standing

❧

Read Hebrews 10:1–18

He waits for his enemies to be made his footstool, because by one sacrifice he has made perfect forever those who are being made holy.
Hebrews 10:13–14

How do we know *personally* that we have a perfect standing before God? Because of the witness of the Holy Spirit through the Word (vv. 15–18). The witness of the Spirit is based on the work of the Son and is given through the words of Scripture. The writer (vv. 16–17) quoted Jeremiah 31:33–34, part of a passage he had also quoted in Hebrews 8:7–12. Old covenant worshippers could not say that they "no longer … felt guilty for their sins" (10:2). But new covenant believers *can* say that their sins are remembered *no more* (v. 17). There is "no longer any sacrifice for sin" (v. 18) and no more remembrance of sin!

I once shared a conference with a fine Christian psychiatrist whose lectures were very true to the Word. "The trouble with psychiatry," he told me, "is that it can only deal with symptoms. A psychiatrist can remove a patient's feelings of guilt, but he cannot remove the guilt. It's like a trucker loosening a fender on his truck so he won't hear the motor knock. A patient can end up feeling better, but have two problems instead of one!"

When sinners trust Christ, their sins are all forgiven, the guilt is gone, and the matter is completely settled forever.

❧

Applying God's Truth:

1. Do you fully believe that you have a perfect standing before God? Why or why not?

2. In what specific ways do you feel you are being "made holy"?

3. Is it possible that you might be repeatedly asking forgiveness for a sin that God has already forgiven? If so, how can you put it behind you and move forward in your spiritual life?

Day 22

Hanging On to Hope

❧

Read Hebrews 10:19–23

Let us hold unswervingly to the hope we profess, for he who promised is faithful.
HEBREWS 10:23

The readers of this epistle were being tempted to forsake their confession of Jesus Christ by going back to the old covenant worship. The writer did not exhort them to hold on to their salvation because their security was in Christ and not in themselves. Rather, he invited them to hold fast to "the hope we profess" (v. 23).

We have noted in our study of Hebrews that there is an emphasis on the glorious hope of believers. God is "bringing many sons to glory" (2:10). Believers "share in the heavenly calling" (3:1) and therefore can rejoice in hope (3:6 KJV). *Hope* is one of the main themes of Hebrews 6. We are looking for Christ to return (9:28), and we are seeking that city that is yet to come (13:14).

When we have our hope fixed on Christ, and rely on the faithfulness of God, then we will not waver. Instead of looking back (as the Jews so often did), we should look ahead to the coming of the Lord (10:23–25).

❧

Applying God's Truth:

1. How would you define "the hope [you] profess"?

2. If you became even more sure of the faithfulness of God than you are now, how might your spiritual life be affected?

3. If you knew for sure that Jesus would return two weeks from today, what would you want to do during the next two weeks? Are these things you should be doing *anyway?*

Day 23

Maintaining Togetherness

Read Hebrews 10:24–39

Let us consider how we may spur one another on toward love and good deeds.
Let us not give up meeting together, as some are in the habit of doing, but let us
encourage one another–and all the more as you see the Day approaching.
HEBREWS 10:24–25

Our fellowship with God must never become selfish. We must also fellowship with other Christians in the local assembly. Apparently, some of the wavering believers had been absenting themselves from the church fellowship. It is interesting to note that the emphasis here is not on what believers get from the assembly, but rather on what they *contribute* to the assembly. Faithfulness in church attendance encourages others and provokes them to love and good works.

One of the strong motives for faithfulness is the soon coming of Jesus Christ. In fact, the only other place the Greek word translated "meeting together" (v. 25) is used in the New Testament is in 2 Thessalonians 2:1, where it is translated "gathered" and deals with the coming of Christ.

The three great Christian virtues are evidenced here: *faith* (Heb. 10:22), *hope* (v. 23), and *love* (v. 24). They are the fruit of our fellowship with God in His heavenly sanctuary.

❧

Applying God's Truth:

1. How would you respond to someone who says, "I don't need to go to church; I can worship God just as well out by myself in nature"?

2. What are the primary benefits you receive from group worship? What do you contribute to the group?

3. How can you "spur" other people toward love and good deeds in a positive way—without "getting on their case"?

Day 24

Faith and Consequences

Read Hebrews 11:1–5

> *Faith is being sure of what we hope for and certain of what we do not see.*
>
> HEBREWS 11:1

True biblical faith is *confident obedience to God's Word in spite of circumstances and consequences.* This faith operates quite simply. God speaks, and we hear His Word. We trust His Word and act on it no matter what the circumstances are or what the consequences may be. The circumstances may be impossible and the consequences frightening and unknown, but we obey God's Word just the same and believe He will do what is right and what is best.

The unsaved world does not understand true biblical faith, probably because it sees so little faith in action in the church today. The cynical editor H. L. Mencken defined faith as "illogical belief in the occurrence of the impossible." The world fails to realize that faith is only as good as its object, and the object of faith is *God* (Rom. 4:3, 20–22). Faith is not some "feeling" that we manufacture. It is our total response to what God has revealed in His Word.

The writer of Hebrews makes it clear that faith is a very practical thing (11:3), in spite of what unbelievers say. Faith enables us to understand what God does. Faith enables us to see what others cannot see. As a result, faith enables us to do what others cannot do! Dr. J. Oswald Sanders put it perfectly: "Faith enables the believing soul to treat the future as present and the invisible as seen."

Applying God's Truth:

1. Now that you have read the author's definition of faith, how would you define it in your own words?

2. Based on your definition, what are some of the best ways to increase your faith?

3. On a scale of 1 (least) to 10 (most), to what extent do circumstances and consequences affect your level of faith?

Day 25

Faith Looks Forward

Read Hebrews 11:6–16

Without faith it is impossible to please God, because anyone who comes to him must believe that he exists and that he rewards those who earnestly seek him.

HEBREWS 11:6

Faith looks to the future, for that is where the greatest rewards are found. The people named in this chapter (and those unnamed) did not receive "the things promised" (v. 13), but they had God's witness to their faith that one day they would be rewarded. God's purpose involves Old Testament saints as well as New Testament saints! One day all of us will share that heavenly city that true saints look for by faith (v. 16).

We today should give thanks for these saints of old, for they were faithful during difficult times, and yet *we* are the ones who have received the better blessing. They saw some of these blessings afar off (v. 13), but we enjoy them today through Jesus Christ. If the saints of old had not trusted God and obeyed His will, Israel would have perished, and the Messiah would not have been born.

Without faith it is impossible to please God. But this faith grows as we listen to His Word and fellowship in worship and prayer. Faith is possible to all kinds of believers in all kinds of situations. It is not a luxury for a few "elite saints." It is a necessity for all of God's people.

Lord, increase our faith (Luke 17:5)!

Applying God's Truth:

1. When is your faith the strongest? When does it seem weakest?

2. Why is faith necessary to please God? Shouldn't obedience be enough in itself?

3. What specific steps can you take to increase your faith?

Day 26

Role Models

❧

Read Hebrews 11:17–30

*Abraham reasoned that God could raise the dead.... By faith Isaac
blessed Jacob and Esau.... By faith Jacob, when he was dying, blessed
each of Joseph's sons.... By faith Joseph, when his end was near,
spoke about the exodus of the Israelites from Egypt.*

HEBREWS 11:19–22

In Abraham, Isaac, Jacob, and Joseph, we have four generations of
faith. These men sometimes failed, but they were devoted to God
and trusted His Word. Isaac passed the promises and the blessings
along to Jacob, and Jacob shared them with his twelve sons. Jacob
was a pilgrim, for even as he was dying he leaned on his pilgrim staff
(v. 21).

The faith of Joseph was certainly remarkable. After the way his
family treated him, we would think he would have abandoned his
faith; but instead, it grew stronger. Even the ungodly influence of
Egypt did not weaken his trust in God. Joseph did not use his family,
his job, or his circumstances as an excuse for unbelief.

We have to admire the faith of the patriarchs. They did not
have a complete Bible, and yet their faith was strong. They handed
God's promises down from one generation to another. In spite of
their failures and tests, these men and women believed God, and
He bore witness to their faith. How much more faith you and I
should have!

Applying God's Truth:

1. What biblical characters would you cite as having the greatest levels of faith? Why?

2. Who are you more like: Abraham, Isaac, Jacob, or Joseph? Why?

3. How do you think your own level of faith would have been affected if you had lived in the days prior to Jesus' life—if you had had only the promise of a Savior without the actual fulfillment of the promise?

Day 27

A Change of Lifestyle

Read Hebrews 11:31–40

By faith the prostitute Rahab, because she welcomed the spies,
was not killed with those who were disobedient.
HEBREWS 11:31

Rahab was an alien prostitute, an unlikely person to put faith in the true God of Israel! *She was saved by grace* because the other inhabitants of the city of Jericho were marked out for death by the invading Israelites (Josh. 2:1–14). God in His mercy and grace permitted Rahab to live. But *she was saved by faith.* She protected the Hebrew spies, put the cord in the window as directed (vv. 15–21), apparently won her family to the true faith (v. 13; 6:25), and in every way obeyed the Lord (vv. 17–25).

Not only was Rahab delivered from judgment, but she became a part of the nation of Israel. She married Salmon and gave birth to Boaz, who was an ancestor of King David (Matt. 1:5–6). Imagine a pagan prostitute becoming a part of the ancestry of Jesus Christ (v. 1)! That is what faith can do!

Rahab is certainly a rebuke to unsaved people who give excuses for not trusting Christ. "I don't know very much about the Bible" is an excuse I often hear. Rahab knew very little spiritual truth, but she acted on what she did know. "I am too bad to be saved!" is another excuse. But Rahab was a condemned heathen prostitute! She stands as one of the great women of faith in the Bible.

※

Applying God's Truth:

1. Do you know people similar to Rahab—with bad past or present reputations, yet a real and growing faith in God? How do most Christians relate to such people?

2. What do you think made Rahab different from all the other people in Jericho?

3. Can you think of any well-known people today who testify to pasts as bad as (or even worse than) Rahab's yet who are dynamic models of Christian faith? What can you learn from such people?

Day 28

Losing Weight

❦

Read Hebrews 12:1–6

Since we are surrounded by such a great cloud of witnesses,
let us throw off everything that hinders and the sin that so easily entangles,
and let us run with perseverance the race marked out for us.

HEBREWS 12:1

Athletes used to wear training weights to help them prepare for events. None of the athletes would have actually participated wearing the weights because they would have slowed them down. (The modern analogy is a baseball player who swings a bat with a heavy metal collar before stepping to the plate.) Too much weight would have taxed their endurance.

What are the "weights" we should remove so that we might win the race? Everything that hinders our progress. They might even be "good things" in the eyes of others. Winning athletes do not choose between the good and the bad; they choose between the better and the best.

We should also get rid of "the sin that so easily entangles" (v. 1). Without naming any specific sin, the writer of Hebrews was probably referring to the sin of unbelief. It was unbelief that kept Israel out of the Promised Land (3:16–19), and it is unbelief that hinders us from entering into our spiritual inheritance in Christ. The phrase "by faith" (or "through faith") is used twenty-one times in chapter 11, indicating that it is faith in Christ that enables us to endure.

❧

Applying God's Truth:

1. What are some of the sins that are most likely to "entangle" you as you attempt to make spiritual progress?

2. What are some of the "weights" you are carrying—not necessarily sins—but things that may impede your spiritual growth?

3. What do you need to do to "throw off" the excess "weights" you may be carrying?

Day 29

Love and Discipline

❧

Read Hebrews 12:7–29

No discipline seems pleasant at the time, but painful. Later on, however, it produces a harvest of righteousness and peace for those who have been trained by it.

HEBREWS 12:11

No chastening at the time is pleasant either to parents or their children, but the benefits are profitable. I am sure that few children believe it when their parents say, "This hurts me more than it hurts you." But it is true just the same. The Father does not enjoy having to discipline His children, but the benefits afterward make the chastening an evidence of His love.

What are some of the benefits? For one thing, there is "a harvest of righteousness." Instead of continuing to sin, the children strive to do what is right. There is also peace instead of war. The rebellion ceases, and the children are in a loving fellowship with the Father. Chastening also encourages children to exercise in spiritual matters— the Word of God, prayer, meditation, witnessing, etc. All this leads to a new *joy*.

Of course, the important thing is how God's children respond to His chastening. They can despise it or faint under it (v. 5 KJV), both of which are wrong. They should show reverence to the Father by submitting to His will (v. 9 KJV), using the experience to exercise themselves spiritually.

In the King James Version, verses 12 and 13 sound like a coach's orders to his team: "Lift up your hands. Strengthen those knees.

Get those lazy feet on the track. On your mark, get set, *go*" (author's paraphrase)!

❧

Applying God's Truth:

1. When you think of "discipline," is it usually in a positive or negative context? What are some of the connotations of "discipline"?

2. Why do you discipline yourself in ways that may not be pleasant (dieting, exercise, etc.)? What are the spiritual parallels of such forms of self-discipline?

3. What is the connection between being chastened by God and experiencing joy? Can you give specific examples of this connection in your own life?

Day 30

Contentment That Lasts

❧

Read Hebrews 13

Keep your lives free from the love of money and be content with what you have, because God has said, "Never will I leave you; never will I forsake you."

HEBREWS 13:5

A Christian couple was ministering to believers in Eastern Europe, behind the iron curtain. The couple had brought in Christian literature, blankets, and other necessary items. At the church gathering, the couple assured the believers that Christians in America were praying for believers in Eastern Europe.

"We are happy for that," one believer replied, "but we feel that Christians in America need more prayer than we do. We here in Eastern Europe are suffering, but you in America are very comfortable; and it is always harder to be a good Christian when you are comfortable."

The phrase "love of money" can be applied to a love for *more* of anything. Someone asked millionaire Bernard Baruch, "How much money does it take for a rich man to be satisfied?" Baruch replied, "Just a million more than he has." Covetousness is the desire for more, whether it is needed or not.

Contentment cannot come from material things, for they can never satisfy the heart. Only God can do that. When we have God, we have all we need. The material things of life can decay or be stolen, but God will never leave us or forsake us.

֍

Applying God's Truth:

1. On a scale of 1 (least) to 10 (most), how content would you say you are with the things you have right now?

2. Are any signs of discontent evident in your life (such as worry, complaining, covetousness, etc.)? If so, how do you deal with them?

3. Create an antidote for discontent by completing this sentence: "The next time I begin to experience a sense of discontentment, I will remember that _____, and then I will _____."

Integrity

Thirty Daily Readings from the Book of 1 John

W̶e must be careful to protect our own personal integrity. When integrity goes, then character starts to decay; when character goes, we have lost everything important. No matter what we may possess—money, popularity, talent, friends—if we don't have character, we don't have anything.

But character depends on integrity. People with integrity are people who are honest with themselves, with others, and with God. They don't wear masks, and they don't waste energy pretending to be what they aren't. They are not afraid of what others may find out about them because they have nothing to hide.

The alternative to integrity is hypocrisy, and that eventually leads to duplicity—becoming two persons inside, neither of whom knows the other. Without inner wholeness, we cannot function successfully in life or enjoy all that God wants us to enjoy.

We must cultivate integrity. That means knowing God: God's forgiveness, God's truth, God's church, and God's love. John's first epistle is a guidebook for the kind of personal integrity that comes from a faithful walk with Jesus Christ, what John calls "walk[ing] in the light" (1 John 1:5–7). No shadows—nothing to hide.

As you ponder this letter these next thirty days, you can discover the joyful inner healing that comes from being exposed to the loving light of God's truth and being honest with God. I pray that this will indeed be your experience.

Whoever loves his brother lives in the light, and there is nothing in him to make him stumble.

1 JOHN 2:10

Day 1

Revealing Words

⚜

Read 1 John 1:1

> *That which was from the beginning, which we have heard,*
> *which we have seen with our eyes, which we have looked at and our*
> *hands have touched—this we proclaim concerning the Word of life.*
>
> 1 JOHN 1:1

If you were God, how would you go about revealing yourself to people? How could you tell them about, and give them, the kind of life you wanted them to enjoy?

God has revealed Himself in creation (Rom. 1:20), but creation alone could never tell the whole story of God's love. God has also revealed Himself much more fully in His Word, the Bible. But God's final and most complete revelation is in His Son, Jesus Christ. Jesus said, "Anyone who has seen me has seen the Father" (John 14:9).

Because Jesus is God's revelation of Himself, He has a very special name: "The Word of Life" (1 John 1:1). This same title opens John's gospel: "In the beginning was the Word, and the Word was with God, and the Word was God" (John 1:1).

Why does Jesus Christ have this name? Because Christ is to us what our words are to others. Our words reveal to others just what we think and how we feel. Christ reveals to us the mind and heart of God. He is the living means of communication between God and us. To know Jesus Christ is to know God!

⚜

Applying God's Truth:

1. What are some things you know about God based on His creation? What do you know about Him from reading the Bible?

2. What other things have you determined to be true about God primarily from examining the life of Jesus?

3. Based on your words during the past twenty-four hours, what have you revealed to other people about yourself?

Day 2

Don't Be Fooled by Imitations

Read 1 John 1:2

The life appeared; we have seen it and testify to it, and we proclaim to you the eternal life, which was with the Father and has appeared to us.

1 JOHN 1:2

There are two kinds of children in this world: "the children of God" and "the children of the devil" (3:10). We would think that "children of the devil" would be people who live in gross sin, but such is not always the case. All unbelievers are "children of the devil." They may be moral and even religious; they may be counterfeit Christians. But because they have never been "born of God" (v. 9) and experienced spiritual life personally, they are still Satan's "children."

Counterfeit Christians—and they are common—are something like counterfeit money. Suppose you have a counterfeit bill and actually think it is genuine. You use it to pay for a tank of gas. The gas station manager uses the bill to buy supplies. The supplier uses the bill to pay the grocer. The grocer bundles the bill up with forty-nine other bills and takes it to the bank. And the teller says, "I'm sorry, but *this* bill is a counterfeit."

That bill may have done a lot of good while it was in circulation, but when it arrived at the bank, it was exposed for what it *really* was and put out of circulation.

So it is with counterfeit Christians. They may do many good things in this life, but when they face the final judgment, they will be rejected. Each of us must ask ourselves honestly, "Am I a true child of God, or am I a counterfeit Christian? Have I truly been born of God?"

❦

Applying God's Truth:

1. Was there a time in your life when you were moral, or even religious, yet not a "child of God"? If so, what happened to help you see your situation more clearly?

2. By what characteristics do you identify "counterfeit Christians" with whom you may come into contact?

3. Even when one's Christian commitment is genuine, what are some "counterfeit" behaviors that can affect spiritual growth?

Day 3

Real Life

Read 1 John 1:3

We proclaim to you what we have seen and heard, so that
you also may have fellowship with us. And our fellowship
is with the Father and with his Son, Jesus Christ.

1 JOHN 1:3

When God made us, He made us in His own image (Gen.
1:26–27). This means that we have a personality patterned
after God's. We have a *mind* to think with, a *heart* to feel with, and a
will with which to make decisions. We sometimes refer to these
aspects of our personality as *intellect, emotion,* and *will.*

The life that is real *must involve all the elements of the personality.*

Most people are dissatisfied today because their total personality has never been controlled by something real and meaningful.
When people are born of God through faith in Christ, God's Spirit
comes into their life to live there forever. As they have fellowship
with God in reading and studying the Bible and in prayer, the Holy
Spirit is able to control their mind, heart, and will. And what happens then?

A Spirit-controlled *mind* knows and understands *truth.*

A Spirit-controlled *heart* feels *love.*

A Spirit-controlled *will* inclines to *obedience.*

John wants to impress this fact on us, and that is why he uses a
series of contrasts in his letter: truth versus lies, love versus hatred,
and obedience versus disobedience. There is no middle ground in the
life that is real. We must be on one side or on the other.

This, then, is the life that is real. It was revealed in Christ; it was experienced by those who trusted in Christ; and it can be shared today by those who are in Christ.

⁂

Applying God's Truth:

1. Of your own intellect, emotion, and will, which would you say is most in need of further development?

2. Which of the three aspects of personality do you find hardest to submit to God? Why?

3. In each of the three areas, what is one thing you can do this week to give the Holy Spirit more control?

Day 4

Walk On

Read 1 John 1:5–7

If we walk in the light, as [God] is in the light, we have fellowship with one another, and the blood of Jesus, his Son, purifies us from all sin.

1 JOHN 1:7

Every form of life has its enemies. Insects have to watch out for hungry birds, and birds must keep an eye on hungry cats and dogs. Even human beings have to dodge automobiles and fight off germs.

The life that is real also has an enemy, and we read about it in this section. This enemy is *sin*. John illustrates his theme by using the contrast between light and darkness: God is light; sin is darkness.

The New Testament calls the Christian life a "walk." This *walk* begins with a step of faith when people trust Christ as their Savior. But salvation is not the end—it is only the beginning—of spiritual life. "Walking" involves progress, and Christians are supposed to advance in the spiritual life. Just as a child must learn to walk and must overcome many difficulties in doing so, a Christian must learn to "walk in the light." And the fundamental difficulty involved here is this matter of *sin*.

Applying God's Truth:

1. What sins have proved to be most threatening and powerful to you in the past?

2. When you identify a recurring sin in your life, how do you deal with it? Can you think of any potential sin in your life right now that needs attention?

3. Do you agree that "walk" is a good description of your spiritual progress? If not, what other word would you choose? (Crawl? Sprint? Jog? Stand still? etc.)

Day 5

Self-Deception

※

Read 1 John 1:8–9

*If we claim to be without sin, we deceive ourselves
and the truth is not in us.*

1 JOHN 1:8

Dishonest believers lose fellowship with God and with God's people. As a result, prayer becomes an empty form to them. Worship is a dull routine. They become critical of other Christians and start staying away from church.

A group of church members was discussing the new pastor.

"For some reason," said one man, "I really don't feel at ease with him. I believe he's a good man, all right—but something seems to stand between us."

Another member replied, "Yes, I think I know what you mean. I used to have that same problem with him, but now I don't have it anymore. The pastor and I have great fellowship."

"What did he do to make things better?"

"He didn't do anything," said the friend. "*I* did the changing."

"*You* did the changing?"

"Yes, I decided to be open and honest about things, the way our pastor is. You see, there isn't one stain of hypocrisy in his life, and there was so much pretending in my life that we just didn't make it together. He and I both knew I was a phony. Since I've started to live an honest Christian life, *everything* is better."

⁂

Applying God's Truth:

1. Most people never *verbally* claim to be "without sin," so how can you tell when others are being dishonest with themselves?

2. When your own praying becomes empty and worship becomes dull, what do you do to get back "on track"?

3. When fellow Christians criticize you, do you consider they may be going through a personal spiritual problem and "cut them some slack"? What are some recent examples of conflict where this might have been the case?

Day 6

Motives for Obedience

❦

Read 1 John 2:1–6

If anyone obeys his word, God's love is truly made complete in him.
1 JOHN 2:5

Obedience to God's Word is proof of our love for Him. There are three motives for obedience. We can obey because we *have* to, because we *need* to, or because we *want* to.

Slaves obey because they *have* to. If they don't obey, they will be punished. Employees obey because they *need* to. They may not enjoy their work, but they do enjoy getting their paycheck! They need to obey because they have a family to feed and clothe. But Christians are to obey their heavenly Father because they *want* to—for the relationship between them and God is one of love: "If you love me, you will obey what I command" (John 14:15).

This is the way we learned obedience when we were children. First, we obeyed because we *had* to. If we didn't obey, we were spanked! But as we grew up, we discovered that obedience meant enjoyment and reward, so we started obeying because it met certain *needs* in our lives. And it was a mark of real maturity when we started obeying because of *love*.

"Baby Christians" must constantly be warned or rewarded. Mature Christians listen to God's Word and obey it simply because they love Him.

※

Applying God's Truth:

1. What are some laws you obey primarily because you have to? What are some you obey because you need to?

2. What are some of *God's* commands you obey primarily out of obligation? Which do you obey because of the benefits you receive?

3. Of the things that came to mind in both of the previous questions, how do you think you might eventually learn to obey the laws/commands out of genuine personal *desire?*

Day 7

Something Old, Something New

Read 1 John 2:7–8

> *I am not writing you a new command but an old one....*
> *Yet I am writing you a new command.*
> 1 JOHN 2:7–8

The Christian life—the life that is real—is a beautiful blending of "something old, something new." The Holy Spirit takes the "old things" and makes them "new things" in our experience. When we stop to think about it, the Holy Spirit never grows old! He is always young! And He is the only person on earth today who was here centuries ago when Jesus lived, taught, died, and rose again. He is the only one who can take "old truth" and make it fresh and new in our daily experience at this present time.

There are other exciting truths in the rest of John's letter, but if we fail to obey in the matter of love, the rest of the letter may well be "darkness" to us. Perhaps the best thing we can do, right *now,* is to search our hearts to see if we hold anything against a fellow believer or if someone has anything against us (vv. 9–11). The life that is real is an honest life—and it is a life of *doing,* not merely *saying.* It is a life of active love in Christ. This means forgiveness, kindness, longsuffering. But it also means joy and peace and victory.

The love life is the only life, because it is the life that is real!

Applying God's Truth:

1. What are some elements of your "old" life that God made new after you became a Christian?

2. Are you currently involved in an unresolved conflict? If so, what steps can you take to try to deal with the matter?

3. Can you think of anything you might be *saying* that you aren't actually *doing*? Can you foresee any potential problems if your actions don't soon begin to support your words?

Day 8

Two "New"s? (Who Knew)

❧❧❧

Read 1 John 2:8

I am writing you a new command; its truth is seen in him and you,
because the darkness is passing and the true light is already shining.

1 JOHN 2:8

The Greeks had two different words for *new*—one meant "new in time," and the other meant "new in quality." For example, we would use the first word to describe the latest car, a recent model. But if we purchased a car that was so revolutionary that it was *radically* different, we would use the second word—new in quality.

The commandment to love one another is not new in time, but it is new in character. Because of Jesus Christ, the old commandment to "love one another" (John 13:34) has taken on new meaning.

It is important that we understand the meaning of Christian love. It is not a shallow sentimental emotion that we Christians try to "work up" so we can get along with each other. It is a matter of the *will* rather than an *emotion*—an affection for and attraction to certain persons. It is a matter of determining—of making up our mind—that we will allow God's love to reach others through us and then of acting toward them in loving ways. We are not to act "as *if* we loved them," but *because* we love them. This is not hypocrisy—it is obedience to God.

Perhaps the best explanation of Christian love is 1 Corinthians 13. You should read a modern translation of this chapter to get the full force of its message: The Christian life without love is *nothing*.

❦

Applying God's Truth:

1. How do you think Jesus' coming to earth affected the way people defined "love"?

2. Have you recently experienced love you would consider "new in quality" or "fresh"? How would you describe it to a friend?

3. In what ways is love a matter of the will for you? Give some specific examples.

Day 9

Lighten Up

❧

Read 1 John 2:9–11

Whoever loves his brother lives in the light, and there
is nothing in him to make him stumble.

1 JOHN 2:10

It is bad enough when unloving believers hurt themselves (v. 9), but when they start to hurt *others* the situation is far more serious. It is *serious* to walk in the darkness. It is *dangerous* to walk in the darkness when stumbling blocks are in the way! Unloving believers stumble themselves, and in addition they cause others to stumble.

A man who was walking down a dark street one night saw a pin-point of light coming toward him in a faltering way. He thought perhaps the person carrying the light was ill or drunk, but as he drew nearer he could see a man carrying a flashlight and a *white cane*.

"Why would a blind man be carrying a light?" the man wondered, and then he decided to ask.

The blind man smiled. "I carry my light, not so I can see, but so that *others* can see me. I cannot help being blind," he said, "but I can help being a stumbling block."

The best way to help other Christians not to stumble is to love them. Love makes us stepping-stones; hatred (or any of its "cousins," such as envy or malice) makes us stumbling blocks. It is important that we Christians exercise love in a local church, or else there will always be problems and disunity. If we are falling over each other, instead of lifting each other higher, we will never become a truly happy spiritual family.

※

Applying God's Truth:

1. In what ways do believers harm themselves when they "walk in the darkness"?

2. How can believers who become stumbling blocks hurt *others?*

3. For each of the answers that came to mind in the previous questions, how can love act as an antidote to those harmful things?

Day 10

The Love God Hates

⚜

Read 1 John 2:12–15

> *Do not love the world or anything in the world. If anyone*
> *loves the world, the love of the Father is not in him.*
>
> 1 JOHN 2:15

J ohn's epistle has reminded us to exercise love (vv. 7–11)—the right
kind of love. Now it warns us that there is a *wrong* kind of love, a
love God hates. This is love for what the Bible calls "the world."

The New Testament word "world" has at least three different
meanings. It sometimes means the *physical* world, the *earth*. It also
means the *human* world, *mankind*. But the warning, "Do not love the
world," is not about the world of nature or the world of people. We
Christians ought to appreciate the beauty and usefulness of the earth
God has made, since He "richly provides us with everything for our
enjoyment" (1 Tim. 6:17). And we certainly ought to love people—not
only our friends, but even our enemies (Matt. 5:44; Luke 6:27, 35).

This "world" named here as our enemy is an invisible *spiritual
system* opposed to God and Christ. "The world," in the Bible, is
Satan's system for opposing the work of Christ on earth. It is the very
opposite of what is godly (1 John 2:16) and holy and spiritual.

We believers are somewhat like scuba divers. The water is not our
natural habitat, for we are not equipped for life in (or under) it. When
we go underwater, we have to take special equipment with us so that
we can breathe.

Likewise, were it not for the Holy Spirit's living within us and the spiritual resources we have in prayer, Christian fellowship, and the Word, we could never "make it" here on earth.

❧

Applying God's Truth:

1. Based on the author's definition of the "world," what are some "worldly" things you need to watch out for?

2. Do you think the best solution to the threat of worldliness is to remove yourself completely from anything that is worldly? Explain.

3. What are some things you have done during the past week to combat the influence of worldliness in your life?

Day 11

Slow and Steady Loses the Race

⁂

Read 1 John 2:16

> *Everything in the world—the cravings of sinful man, the lust of his eyes and the boasting of what he has and does—comes not from the Father but from the world.*
>
> 1 JOHN 2:16

As Christians, the world appeals to us through "the lust of the flesh, and the lust of the eyes, and the pride of life" (KJV). And once the world takes over in one of these areas, we soon realize it. We lose our enjoyment of the Father's love and our desire to do the Father's will. The Bible becomes boring and prayer a difficult chore. Even Christian fellowship may seem empty and disappointing. It is not that there is something wrong with others; however, what is wrong is our worldly heart.

It is important to note that none of us become worldly all of a sudden. Worldliness creeps up on us; it is a gradual process. Worldliness rears its ugly head in many subtle and unrecognized forms. Sometimes we tend to idolize great athletes, musicians, TV or movie stars, or political leaders who profess to be Christians—as if these individuals were able to be of special help to almighty God. Or we cater to wealthy and "influential" persons in our local church, as if God's work would fold up without their goodwill or financial backing. *Many* forms of worldliness do not involve reading the wrong books and indulging in "carnal" amusements.

❧

Applying God's Truth:

1. What are some worldly appeals you have recently faced in each of these categories: (1) sinful cravings, (2) the lust of the eyes, and (3) pride/boasting?

2. If worldliness is a gradual process, what do you think is the *first* symptom?

3. Are there any people you hold in such high esteem that it may approach worldly idolization? How can you prevent yourself from going too far in your devotion and admiration?

Day 12

Avoiding Oblivion

Read 1 John 2:17

> *The world and its desires pass away, but the man*
> *who does the will of God lives forever.*
>
> 1 JOHN 2:17

E very great nation in history has become decadent and has finally been conquered by another nation. There is no reason why we should suppose that *our* nation will be an exception. Some nineteen world civilizations in the past have slipped into oblivion. There is no reason why we should think that our present civilization will endure forever. "Change and decay in all around I see," wrote Henry F. Lyte (1793–1847); and if our civilization is not eroded by change and decay, it will certainly be swept away and replaced by a new order of things at the coming of Christ, which could happen at any time.

Slowly but inevitably, and perhaps sooner than even we Christians think, the world is passing away; but those who do God's will abide forever. Long after this world system, with its vaunted culture, its proud philosophies, its egocentric intellectualism, and its godless materialism, has been forgotten, and long after this planet has been replaced by the new heavens and the new earth (Rev. 21:1), God's faithful servants will remain—sharing the glory of God for all eternity.

And this prospect is not limited to Moody, Spurgeon, Luther, or Wesley and their likes—it is open to each and every humble believer. If you are trusting Christ, it is for *you.*

❦

Applying God's Truth:

1. How do you think your nation will be different fifty years from now? (Consider potential geographic changes, economic considerations, spiritual condition, and so forth.)

2. Considering that the world system is eventually going to slip into oblivion, what things are you regularly involved in that may prove to be counterproductive or a waste of time?

3. If you are expecting to "[share] the glory of God for all eternity," what things are you doing now to prepare for such an encounter?

Day 13

Sincerely Wrong

Read 1 John 2:18–20

You have an anointing from the Holy One,
and all of you know the truth.
1 JOHN 2:20

It makes no difference what you believe, just as long as you are sincere!" That statement expresses the personal philosophy of many people today, but it is doubtful whether most of those who make it have really thought it through. Is "sincerity" the magic ingredient that makes something *true?* If so, then we ought to be able to apply it to any area of life and not only to religion.

A nurse in a city hospital gives some medicine to a patient, and the patient becomes violently ill. The nurse is sincere, but the medicine is wrong, and the patient almost dies.

A man hears noises in the house one night and decides a burglar is at work. He gets his gun and shoots the "burglar," who turns out to be his daughter! Unable to sleep, she has gotten up for a bite to eat. She ends up the victim of her father's "sincerity."

It takes more than "sincerity" to make something true. Faith in a lie will always cause serious consequences; faith in the truth is never misplaced. *It does make a difference what we believe!* If we want to drive from Chicago to New York, no amount of sincerity will get us there if the highway is taking us to Los Angeles. People who are real build their lives on truth, not superstition or lies. It is impossible to live a real life by believing lies.

❦

Applying God's Truth:

1. When is the last time you can remember feeling strongly about something you were very sincere about, only to eventually discover you were wrong?

2. On a scale of 1 (least) to 10 (most), how strongly would you say you value the truth? (For example, if telling a "white lie" would spare someone some pain, would you still be completely honest?)

3. What connections have you discovered between faith and truth in your own life?

Day 14

Discern as You Learn

❦

Read 1 John 2:21–25

Who is the liar? It is the man who denies that Jesus is the Christ....
No one who denies the Son has the Father; whoever
acknowledges the Son has the Father also.

1 John 2:22–23

We are warned against letting any human being be our teacher, for God has given us the Spirit to teach us His truth. This does not deny the office of human teachers in the church (Eph. 4:11–12), but it means that under the guidance of the Spirit we must test the teaching of people as we search the Bible for ourselves (1 John 4:1; Acts 17:11).

A missionary to Native Americans was in Los Angeles with an Indian friend who was a new Christian. As they walked down the street, they passed a man on the corner who was preaching with a Bible in his hand. The missionary knew the man represented a cult, but the Indian saw only the Bible. He stopped to listen to the sermon.

"I hope my friend doesn't get confused," the missionary thought to himself, and he began to pray. In a few minutes the Indian turned away from the meeting and joined his missionary friend.

"What did you think of that preacher?" the missionary asked.

"All the time he was talking," exclaimed the Indian, "something in my heart kept saying, 'Liar! Liar!'"

That "something" in his heart was "Someone"—the Holy Spirit of God! The Spirit guides us into the truth and helps us to recognize error (John 16:13). This anointing of God is "no lie," because "the Spirit is the truth" (1 John 5:6).

※

Applying God's Truth:

1. How do you respond to attempts by cult members or other false teachers who approach you with a distorted version of the truth of the gospel?

2. Can you think of a specific time when the Holy Spirit alerted you to a cleverly disguised falsehood being promoted by some?

3. How hard do you work to keep from being taken in by someone? Are you quick to let someone speak for you, or do you do a lot of careful examination of Scripture on your own?

Day 15

Truth or You-Know-What

❧

Read 1 John 2:26–29

*Now, dear children, continue in him, so that when he appears
we may be confident and unashamed before him at his coming.*

1 JOHN 2:28

A person who *professes* to be a Christian but does not live in obedience, love, and truth is either deceived or a deceiver. A child bears the nature of an earthly father, and a person who has been "born of God" will reveal the characteristics of the heavenly Father.

A Sunday school class seemed to be having constant problems. The pastor and the superintendent met with the teacher and officers but made no apparent progress. Then, one Sunday morning, the teacher of the class came down the aisle during the closing hymn of the service. "I suppose she wants to dedicate her life to the Lord," the pastor thought.

"Pastor," she said, "I want to confess Christ as my Savior. All these years I thought I was saved, but I wasn't. There was always something lacking in my life. The class problems were my problems, but now they've been solved. Now I *know* I'm saved."

"Examine yourselves to see whether you are in the faith; test yourselves" (2 Cor. 13:5). Does our life bear the marks of obedience, love, and truth? Is our Christian life something *real—genuine—authentic?* Or is it counterfeit?

It is a question of truth—or consequences! And if we do not face the truth, we must suffer the consequences!

Applying God's Truth:

1. Can you think of any professed Christians you suspect to be deceived? Do you know any deceivers? How do you tend to identify such people?

2. What are some of your characteristics that reflect the characteristics of God?

3. What would it take to make your Christian life more real, genuine, and authentic?

Day 16

Ain't Nothing Like the Real Thing

Read 1 John 3:1–3

> *We know that when he appears, we shall be like him,*
> *for we shall see him as he is.*
> 1 JOHN 3:2

The United States Treasury Department has a special group of employees whose job it is to track down counterfeiters. Naturally, these people need to know a counterfeit bill when they see it.

How do they learn to identify fake bills?

Oddly enough, they are not trained by spending hours examining counterfeit money. Rather, they study *the real thing*. They become so familiar with authentic bills that they can spot a counterfeit by looking at it or, often, simply by feeling it.

This is the approach in 1 John 3, which warns us that in today's world there are counterfeit Christians—"children of the devil" (v. 10). But instead of listing the evil characteristics of *Satan's* children, the Scripture gives us a clear description of *God's* children. The contrast between the two is obvious.

Unsaved people (even if they profess to be Christians but are counterfeits) live a life of habitual sin. Sin—especially the sin of unbelief—is the normal thing in their life (Eph. 2:1–3). They have no divine resources to draw upon. Their profession of faith, if any, is not real. True believers do not live in habitual sin. They may *commit* sin—an occasional wrong act—but they will not *practice* sin—make a settled habit of it.

Applying God's Truth:

1. By what means do you identify "counterfeit" Christians?

2. What are some of the habitual sins you have found hardest to eliminate from your life? Why do you think these are such problem areas for you?

3. Since our goal is to "be like [Jesus]," in what areas do you think you are doing fairly well? What areas still need a lot of work?

Day 17

The War Is Over

⁂

Read 1 John 3:4–6

> *No one who lives in him keeps on sinning. No one who*
> *continues to sin has either seen him or known him.*
> 1 JOHN 3:6

For many months after the close of World War II, Japanese troops were discovered hidden in the caves and jungles of the Pacific islands. Some of these stragglers were living like frightened savages; they didn't know the war was over. Once they understood that it was no longer necessary for them to fight, they surrendered.

Christians may rest in the truth that Satan is a defeated enemy. He may still win a few battles here and there, but *he has already lost the war!* Sentence has been pronounced on him, but it will be awhile before the punishment is meted out. People who know Christ and who have been delivered from the bondage of sin through Christ's death on the cross have no desire to obey Satan and live like rebels.

Counterfeit Christians were trying to convince true believers that people could be "saved" and still practice sin. John did not deny that Christians sin, but he *did* deny that Christians can *live in sin*. People who can enjoy deliberate sin and who do not feel convicted or experience God's chastening had better examine themselves to see whether they are really born of God.

❧

Applying God's Truth:

1. In what ways do you live in celebration of the fact that the war with Satan is over and that he has lost?

2. Would any of your actions or attitudes indicate that your victory is in doubt?

3. What would you tell a friend who professed to be a Christian yet claimed to enjoy indulging in a particular sin on a regular basis?

Day 18

Backsliding Is Not Good Exercise

Read 1 John 3:7–10

Do not let anyone lead you astray. He who does what is right is righteous, just as he is righteous. He who does what is sinful is of the devil.

1 JOHN 3:7–8

Unconfessed sin is the first step in what the Bible calls "backsliding"—gradually moving away from a close walk with the Lord into a life filled with the alien world in which believers live.

God's promise "I will cure you of backsliding" (Jer. 3:22) implies that backsliding resembles physical sickness. First is the secret invasion of the body by a disease germ. Then infection follows, and there is a gradual decline: no pep, no appetite, no interest in normal activities. Then comes the collapse!

Spiritual decline works in a similar way. First, sin invades us. Instead of fighting it, we yield to it (James 1:14–15), and infection sets in. A gradual decline follows. We lose our appetite for spiritual things, we become listless and even irritable, and finally we collapse. The only remedy is to confess and forsake our sin and turn to Christ for cleansing and healing.

Our "inner man" (Eph. 3:16 KJV) not only needs food and cleansing, but also needs exercise: "Train yourself to be godly" (1 Tim. 4:7). People who eat but do not exercise will become overweight; people who exercise without eating will kill themselves. There must be proper balance. "Spiritual exercise" for us believers includes sharing

Christ with others, doing good works in Christ's name, and helping to build up other believers.

❦

Applying God's Truth:

1. What would you say was your most recent incident of "backsliding"? Can you identify what caused the initial lack of spiritual momentum?

2. With what have you fed your appetite for spiritual things during this past week?

3. What kinds of spiritual "exercise" have you had this week? Do you think you may need to increase your exercise? If so, what other activities could you add?

Day 19

Killer Instinct

Read 1 John 3:11–15

> *We know that we have passed from death to life, because we love our brothers.... Anyone who hates his brother is a murderer.*
>
> 1 JOHN 3:14–15

A visitor at the zoo was chatting with the keeper of the lion house. "I have a cat at home," said the visitor, "and your lions act just like my cat. Look at them sleeping so peacefully! It seems a shame that you have to put those beautiful creatures behind bars."

"My friend," the keeper laughed, "these may look like your cat, but their disposition is radically different. There's murder in their hearts. You'd better be glad the bars are there."

The only reason some people have never actually murdered anyone is because of the "bars" that have been put up: the fear of arrest and shame, the penalties of the law, and the possibility of death. But we are all going to be judged by "the law of liberty" (James 2:12 KJV). The question is not so much, "What did you *do?*" but "What did you *want* to do? What would you have done if you had been at liberty to do as you pleased?" This is why Jesus equated hatred with murder (Matt. 5:21–26) and lust with adultery (vv. 27–30).

This does not mean, of course, that hatred in the heart does the same amount of damage or involves the same degree of guilt as actual murder. Our neighbors would rather we hate them than kill them! But in God's sight, hatred is the moral equivalent of murder, and if left unbridled, it leads to murder.

❦

Applying God's Truth:

1. What are some of the emotions you have recently felt or expressed that you realized were stronger than you thought? Could such emotions "mask" deeper feelings?

2. What are some "bars" that keep you from acting on all of your feelings?

3. If you were judged today for all the things you *wanted* to do during the past week, how would you do? After you eliminate most of the sinful actions from your life, how can you get rid of the sinful *attitudes* as well?

Day 20

Good and Cheap

❧

Read 1 John 3:16–17

This is how we know what love is: Jesus Christ laid down his life for us.
And we ought to lay down our lives for our brothers.

1 JOHN 3:16

In these days of multiplied social agencies, it is easy for us Christians to forget our obligations: "Let us do good to all people, especially to those who belong to the family of believers" (Gal. 6:10).

This "doing good" need not be in terms of money or material supplies. It may include personal service and the giving of ourselves to others. There are many individuals in our churches who lack love and who would welcome our friendship.

A young mother admitted, in a testimony meeting, that she never seemed to find time for her own personal devotions. She had several little children to care for, and the hours melted away.

Imagine her surprise when two of the ladies from the church appeared at her front door.

"We've come to take over," they explained. "You go into the bedroom and get started on your devotions." After several days of this kind of help, the young mother was able to develop her devotional life so that the daily demands on her time no longer upset her.

If we want to experience and enjoy the love of God in our own hearts, we must love others, even to the point of sacrifice.

Applying God's Truth:

1. What would you consider the most sacrificial act you have done for someone else?

2. What are some "little" ways you could help others in your church, family, or neighborhood this week?

3. What are some things you wish people would do for you occasionally? Have you ever made your needs known to others?

Day 21

At Ease

Read 1 John 3:18–24

This then is how we know that we belong to the truth, and how we set our hearts at rest in his presence whenever our hearts condemn us. For God is greater than our hearts, and he knows everything.

1 JOHN 3:19–20

A "condemning heart" is one that robs us of peace. An "accusing conscience" is another way to describe it. Sometimes the heart accuses us wrongly, because it "is deceitful above all things and beyond cure. Who can understand it?" (Jer. 17:9). The answer to that question is, "God understands the heart!"

We must be careful lest the Devil accuse us and rob us of our confidence (Rev. 12:10). Once we confess our sin, and it is forgiven, we need not allow it to accuse us anymore.

We should not treat sin lightly, but we should not be harder on ourselves than God is. There is a morbid kind of self-examination and self-condemnation that is not spiritual. If we are practicing genuine love for the brethren, our heart must be right before God, for the Holy Spirit would not "shed abroad" His love in us (Rom. 5:5 KJV) if there were habitual sin in our heart. When we grieve the Spirit we "turn off" the supply of God's love (Eph. 4:30—5:2).

Applying God's Truth:

1. Have you done something that God has forgiven, but that you

are still condemning yourself for? What do you need to do to experience His forgiveness more fully?

2. In what ways does the Devil "accuse [you] and rob [you] of [your] confidence"?

3. You don't want to be harder on yourself than God is. Is it possible that you may be harder on *someone else* than God is? If so, what do you need to do for the person(s) involved?

Day 22

Back to (God's) Nature

❧

Read 1 John 4:1–8

> *Dear friends, let us love one another, for love comes from God.*
> *Everyone who loves has been born of God and knows God.*
> *Whoever does not love does not know God, because God is love.*
>
> 1 JOHN 4:7–8

Love is a valid test of our fellowship and our relationship because "God is love." Love is a part of the very being and nature of God. If we are united to God through faith in Christ, we share His nature. And since His nature is love, love is the test of the reality of our spiritual life.

A navigator depends on a compass to help him determine his course. But why a compass? Because it shows him his directions. And why does the compass point north? Because it is so constituted that it responds to the magnetic field that is part of the earth's makeup. The compass is responsive to the nature of the earth.

So it is with Christian love. The nature of God is love. And a person who knows God and has been born of God will respond to God's nature. As a compass naturally points north, a believer will naturally practice love, because love is the nature of God. This love will not be a forced response; it will be a natural response. A believer's love for the brethren will be proof of his sonship and fellowship.

❧

Applying God's Truth:

1. If God is love—if that is His nature—how does that attribute affect His other attributes (justice, power, knowledge, etc.)?

2. Where do you think most Christians fall short of reflecting the complete love of God?

3. If God's complete love were indicated by due north on a compass, what direction would your own personal compass read? (How far off would you be?)

Day 23

Tell and Show

Read 1 John 4:9–11

> *This is love: not that we loved God, but that he loved us and
> sent his Son as an atoning sacrifice for our sins. Dear friends,
> since God so loved us, we also ought to love one another.*
>
> 1 JOHN 4:10–11

A Salvation Army worker found a derelict woman alone on the
street and invited her to come into the chapel for help, but
the woman refused to move. The female worker assured her: "We
love you and want to help you. God loves you. Jesus died for you."
But the woman did not budge.

As if on divine impulse, the army worker leaned over and kissed
the woman on the cheek, taking her into her arms. The woman began
to sob and, like a child, was led into the chapel, where she ultimately
trusted Christ.

"You *told* me that God loved me," she said later, "but it wasn't
until you showed me that God loved me that I wanted to be saved."

Jesus did not simply preach the love of God; He proved it by giving His life on the cross. He expects His followers to do likewise. If
we abide in Christ, we will abide in His love. If we abide in His love,
we must share this love with others. Whenever we share this love, it
is proof in our own hearts that we are abiding in Christ. In other
words, as Christians there is no separation between our inner life and
our outer life.

❦

Applying God's Truth:

1. Jesus was an excellent teacher, but what do you think He would have accomplished if He had only taught and had not ministered to people and died on the cross for them?

2. Did you become a Christian because of something you heard, something you saw in the life of another person, or a combination of the two? How do you think most people are attracted to the gospel of Christ?

3. Whom have you told about the love of God recently? To whom have you *shown* it?

Day 24

Aha!

❦

Read 1 John 4:12–16

If anyone acknowledges that Jesus is the Son of God,
God lives in him and he in God.

1 JOHN 4:15

In order to save money, a college drama class purchased only a few scripts of a play and cut them up into the separate parts. The director gave each player his or her individual part in order and then started to rehearse the play. But nothing went right. After an hour of missed cues and mangled sequences, the cast gave up.

At that point, the director sat all the actors on the stage and said: "Look, I'm going to read the entire play to you, so don't any of you say a word." He read the entire script aloud, and when he was finished, one of the actors said:

"So that's what it was all about!"

And when the players understood the entire story, they were able to fit their parts together and have a successful rehearsal.

When we read 1 John 4:12–16, we feel like saying, "So that's what it's all about!" Here we discover what God had in mind when He devised His great plan of salvation.

❦

Applying God's Truth:

1. Are there any "pieces" of your faith that you don't fully

understand? If so, whom can you talk to this week to help you see how they fit into the "entire story"?

2. Besides Jesus' sacrificial death on the cross, what are some other things He does (or did) to prove that God loves us?

3. If a stranger watched you for a week, could that individual tell that "God lives in [you]"? Why or why not?

Day 25

Overcoming Fear

❧

Read 1 John 4:17–19

There is no fear in love. But perfect love drives out fear, because fear has to do with punishment. The one who fears is not made perfect in love.

1 JOHN 4:18

Two brand-new words come into John's vocabulary here: "fear" and "punishment." And this passage is written to *believers!* Is it possible that Christians can actually live in fear? Yes, unfortunately, many professed believers experience both fear and torment day after day. And the reason is that they are not growing in the love of God.

If people are afraid, it is because of something in the past that haunts them, or something in the present that upsets them, or something in the future that they feel threatens them. Or it may be a combination of all three. Believers in Jesus Christ do not have to fear the past, present, or future; for they have experienced the love of God, and this love is being perfected in them day by day.

God wants His children to live in an atmosphere of love and confidence, not fear and potential punishment. Immature Christians are tossed between fear and love; mature Christians rest in God's love.

A growing confidence in the presence of God is one of the first evidences that our love for God is maturing.

❧

Applying God's Truth:

1. Isn't "fear of the Lord" something we are supposed to have? Is

there a difference between "fear of the Lord" and being afraid of God and what He might do to us?

2. Do you know Christians who seem to live in constant fear and/or dread of potential punishment? How might you be able to help them?

3. What can *you* do this week to rest more securely in God's love?

Day 26

Pleasing Priorities

꧁꧂

Read 1 John 4:20–21

Anyone who does not love his brother, whom he has seen,
cannot love God, whom he has not seen.

1 JOHN 4:20

When our hearts are confident toward God, there is no need for us to pretend, either to God or to other people. If we lack confidence with God, we will also lack confidence with God's people. Part of the torment that fear generates is the constant worry, "How much do others really know about me?" But when we have confidence with God, this fear is gone, and we can face both God and people without worry.

"How many members do you have in your church?" a visitor asked the pastor.

"Somewhere near a thousand," the pastor replied.

"That certainly is a lot of people to try to please!" the visitor exclaimed.

"Let me assure you, my friend, that I have never tried to please all my members or even some of them," the pastor said with a smile. "I aim to please one person—the Lord Jesus Christ. If I am right with Him, then everything should be right between me and my people."

Immature Christians who are not growing in their love for God may think they have to impress others with their "spirituality." This mistake turns them into liars! They are professing something that they are not really practicing; they are playing a role instead of living a life.

Applying God's Truth:

1. Who are the people you are reluctant to "be yourself" in front of? What's the worst that could happen if they "really knew about you"?

2. What do you do to encourage others to be more comfortable around you?

3. Do you think it is wrong to want to please or impress people from time to time? If not, what potential problems might arise out of such a desire to please others?

Day 27

The Secret of Joyful Obedience

⚜

Read 1 John 5:1–3

> *This is love for God: to obey his commands.*
> *And his commands are not burdensome.*
>
> 1 JOHN 5:3

E verything in creation—except man—obeys the will of God. "Lightning and hail, snow and clouds, stormy winds … do his bidding" (Ps. 148:8). In the book of Jonah, we see the winds and waves, and even the fish, obeying God's commands, but the prophet stubbornly wanted his own way.

Disobedience to God's will is a tragedy—but so is reluctant, grudging obedience. God does not want us to disobey Him, but neither does He want us to obey Him out of fear or necessity. What Paul wrote about *giving* also applies to *living:* "not reluctantly or under compulsion, for God loves a cheerful giver" (2 Cor. 9:7).

What is the secret of *joyful* obedience? It is to recognize that obedience is a family matter. We are serving a loving Father and helping our brothers and sisters in Christ. We have been born of God; we love God, and we love God's children. And we demonstrate this love by keeping God's commandments.

⚜

Applying God's Truth:

1. Can you think of anything you have done this week that was clearly disobedient to one of God's commands?

2. Can you think of anything you have done this week to obey God's commands, but that you did grudgingly or reluctantly? If so, why were you so resistant?

3. What are three specific things you would be willing to try this week to attempt to make your obedience more joyful?

Day 28

Friends in High Places

❧

Read 1 John 5:4–5

Who is it that overcomes the world?
Only he who believes that Jesus is the Son of God.
1 JOHN 5:5

A Civil War veteran used to wander from place to place, begging a bed and bite to eat and always talking about his friend, "Mr. Lincoln." Because of his injuries, he was unable to hold a steady job. But as long as he could keep going, he would chat about his beloved president.

"You say you knew Mr. Lincoln," a skeptical bystander retorted one day. "I'm not so sure you did. Prove it!"

The old man replied, "Why, sure, I can prove it. In fact, I have a piece of paper here that Mr. Lincoln himself signed and gave to me."

From his old wallet, the man took out a much-folded piece of paper and showed it to the man.

"I'm not much for reading," he apologized, "but I know that's Mr. Lincoln's signature."

"Man, do you know what you have here?" one of the spectators asked. "You have a generous federal pension authorized by President Lincoln. You don't have to walk around like a poor beggar! Mr. Lincoln has made you rich!"

To paraphrase what John wrote: "You Christians do not have to walk around defeated, because Jesus Christ has made you victors! He has defeated every enemy, and you share His victory. Now, by *faith,* claim His victory."

※

Applying God's Truth:

1. What does it mean to you that you have "overcome the world"?

2. In what ways do you occasionally feel defeated by the events you face in life?

3. You can "claim victory" by faith, but what will it take for you to truly *feel* victorious?

Day 29

Confident of Answers

❧

Read 1 John 5:6–15

> *This is the confidence we have in approaching God:*
> *that if we ask anything according to his will, he hears us.*
>
> 1 JOHN 5:14

What breathing is to a physical person, prayer is to a spiritual person. Prayer is not only the utterance of the lips; it is also the desire of the heart. "Pray continually" (1 Thess. 5:17) does not mean that we Christians should always be saying an audible prayer. We are not heard for our "much speaking" (Matt. 6:7 KJV). No, "pray continually" suggests the attitude of the heart as well as the words of the lips. If our heart is fixed on Christ and we are trying to glorify Him, we are praying even when we are not conscious of it.

Charles Haddon Spurgeon, the famous preacher, was working hard on a message but was unable to complete it. It grew late, and his wife said, "Why don't you go to bed. I'll wake you up early, and you can finish your sermon in the morning."

Spurgeon dozed off and in his sleep began to preach the sermon that was giving him so much trouble! His wife wrote down what he said, and the next morning gave her preacher-husband the notes.

"Why, that's exactly what I wanted to say!" exclaimed the surprised preacher. The message had been in his heart; it had simply needed expression. So it is with prayer: If we are abiding in Christ, the very desires of our heart are heard by God whether we voice them or not.

❧

Applying God's Truth:

1. How do you determine whether you are praying "according to [God's] will"?

2. During the times when it seems that God isn't hearing you, do you continue to pray faithfully? Or do you get discouraged during those times? How can you maintain a positive outlook even when your immediate feelings don't support it?

3. What are some of the "desires of your heart" (Ps. 37:4) that you haven't expressed to God in a while? Are you confident enough to ask Him again for those things?

Day 30

For Real

❧

Read 1 John 5:16–21

We are in him who is true—even in his Son Jesus Christ.
He is the true God and eternal life.

1 JOHN 5:20

The world boasts of enlightenment, but Christians walk in the *real* light because "God is light" (1:5). The world talks about love, but it knows nothing of the *real* love Christians experience because "God is love" (4:8, 16). The world displays its wisdom and learning, but Christians live in truth because the Spirit is truth (John 14:17; 15:26; 16:13). God is light, love, and truth; and these together make a life that is *real*.

"But it makes no difference what people believe so long as they are sincere!"

This popular excuse hardly needs refutation. Does it make any difference what the pharmacist believes, or the surgeon, or the chemist? It makes all the difference in the world.

> *Shed a tear for Jimmy Brown;*
> *Poor Jimmy is no more.*
> *For what he thought was H_2O*
> *Was H_2SO_4.*

(H_2O is water. H_2SO_4 is sulfuric acid.)

Christians have "turned to God from idols to serve the living and true God" (1 Thess. 1:9). Idols are dead, but Christ is the living God. Idols are false, but Christ is the true God. This is the secret of the life that is real!

So John's admonition "Keep yourselves from idols" (1 John 5:21) can be paraphrased, "Watch out for the imitation and the artificial and be real!"

✣

Applying God's Truth:

1. What is the most significant thing you have learned (or reviewed) by going through the book of 1 John?

2. What is an evidence from your own life that God is light? Love? Truth?

3. What are three specific things you can do to begin to live a more real life from this moment forward?